MORE MEALS
in minutes

SUE ASHWORTH

SIMON & SCHUSTER
A VIACOM COMPANY

First published in Great Britain by Simon & Schuster, 1997
A Viacom Company

Copyright © 1997, Weight Watchers (UK) Ltd

Simon & Schuster Ltd
West Garden Place
Kendal Street
London W2 2AQ

Weight Watchers and 1,2,3 Success are Trademarks of Weight Watchers
International Inc. and are used under its control by Weight Watchers (UK) Ltd.

Design: Green Moore Lowenhoff
Cover design: Jane Humphrey
Typesetting: Stylize
Photography: Sue Atkinson
Styling: Sue Russell
Food preparation: Jane Stevenson

Weight Watchers Publications Executive: Juliet Hudson
Weight Watchers Publications Assistant: Celia Whiston

A CIP catalogue record is available from the British Library

ISBN 0-68481-928-7

Printed and bound in Italy by Rotolito Lombarda S.p.A.

Pictured on the front cover: *Chinese Pork and Noodle Stir-Fry (page 47)*

Pictured on the back cover: *Continental Salad* and *Chick-pea and Tuna Salad (page 20)*

Recipe notes:
Egg size is medium, unless otherwise stated.
Vegetables are medium-sized, unless otherwise stated.
The Points and Calorie values are for the main recipes only; remember to add extra
Points or Calories for the accompaniments.
It is important to use proper measuring spoons, not cutlery, for spoon measures.
1 tablespoon = 15 ml; 1 teaspoon = 5 ml.
Dried herbs can be substituted for fresh ones, but the flavour may not always
be as good. Halve the fresh-herb quantity stated in the recipe.

Vegetarian recipes:

 shows the recipe is vegetarian.

Contents

Introduction

Today's busy lifestyles demand quick-and-easy answers to the question of what to eat. When you add the need to lose weight or maintain a healthy diet, it may seem impossible to do it all. But these recipes prove that it isn't! It *is* possible to eat healthy fast food that tastes great and is easy to prepare and cook at home.

Whether you are following Weight Watchers *1,2,3 Success*™ Programme or simply have an interest in healthy eating, you'll find *More Meals in Minutes* full of tasty and truly satisfying recipes which don't take ages to make. By using low-fat foods and a few tricks to reduce the fat and Calories in other foods, along with making the very best of fresh vegetables and fruit, we have come up with an array of exciting recipes that will be a joy to cook: not just once, but over and over again.

One of the secrets of quick meals is a well-stocked store-cupboard, with plenty of versatile basics. It pays to have lots of rice, pasta and quick-cook noodles ready to hand. Have a good supply of easily available convenience foods – frozen, canned or packaged – to give you finished meals that don't take long to prepare. Stock up on your favourite canned fish, vegetables and fruits; canned beans in their many varieties are also excellent for speedy meals. Have a wide variety of spices and dried herbs and, if you have green fingers, try growing fresh herbs yourself. You may find that when you cut down the fat in food, you need a bit more flavour to get real satisfaction, so don't hesitate to spice things up a bit.

Whether you are making meals for yourself, your family or your friends, you are sure to find this cookbook a real kitchen companion. So enjoy the food in *More Meals in Minutes*: Weight Watchers guarantee you'll see the results of a good diet in no time!

Soups

Nothing beats the flavour of home-made soup and it needn't be complicated or time-consuming to make. In fact, it can be almost as simple as opening a can and yet the flavour and nutritive value will be far, far greater!

The recipes in this chapter are simple, yet stylish. Each one would make a delicious light meal in itself, or serve them as starters before something more substantial. What you can be assured of is that once you've tried them, you'll enjoy making these recipes over and over again for yourself, your family, and your friends.

Light Chicken and Vegetable Broth

Serves 4

Preparation and cooking time:
25 minutes
Calories per serving: 35

Freezing: recommended

A light stock with shredded vegetables, chicken and chopped fresh herbs makes a very low-calorie, low-Point soup.

2 chicken stock cubes, dissolved in 900 ml (1½ pints) boiling water
1 bunch of spring onions, sliced finely
1 small carrot, cut in fine strips
1 small leek, shredded
2 tablespoons mixed chopped fresh herbs, e.g. parsley, chives, oregano, thyme, basil, etc.
60 g (2 oz) cooked chicken, shredded finely
salt and freshly ground black pepper
chopped fresh herbs, to garnish

1. Pour the stock into a large saucepan and add the spring onions, carrot and leek. Cover and cook gently for 10 minutes.
2. Add the herbs and the chicken to the saucepan and simmer gently for 5 minutes. Season to taste with salt and pepper.
3. Ladle the soup into warmed bowls and sprinkle each portion with extra chopped herbs.

Cook's note:
Look out for tom yam stock cubes from delicatessen and oriental food suppliers. Use these instead of chicken stock cubes, to lend a fabulous Thai flavour to this soup.

Points per serving: ½
Total Points per recipe: 2

Mexican Bean Broth

Serves 4

Preparation and cooking time:
30 minutes
Calories per serving: 140

Freezing: recommended

Fire up this speedy bean and sweetcorn soup with spicy chilli flakes if you like more flavour.

2 teaspoons vegetable oil
2 garlic cloves, chopped
1 onion, chopped
½ teaspoon dried chilli flakes or powder (optional)
420 g (14 oz) canned chopped tomatoes
2 vegetable stock cubes, dissolved in 900 ml (1½ pints) boiling water
1 tablespoon tomato purée
360 g (12 oz) canned mixed beans, rinsed and drained
180 g (6 oz) canned or frozen sweetcorn
1 tablespoon chopped fresh coriander or parsley (optional)
salt and freshly ground black pepper

1. Heat the oil in a large saucepan and sauté the garlic and onion for about 3 minutes, until softened. Add the chilli flakes or powder (if using) and the tomatoes and bring to the boil.
2. Pour in the stock and add the tomato purée, beans and sweetcorn. Bring back to the boil and leave to simmer, uncovered, for 15 minutes.
3. Add the coriander or parsley (if using) to the soup and season with salt and pepper. Ladle into warm soup bowls and serve at once.

Cook's note:
If you are not keen on chilli flakes or powder, use a teaspoon of dried mixed herbs instead.

Points per serving: 2
Total Points per recipe: 8

Cauliflower and Blue Cheese Soup

Serves 4

Preparation and cooking time:
30 minutes
Calories per serving: 200

Freezing: recommended

V if using vegetarian cheese

Low-fat soft cheese with a little crumbled Stilton gives a delightful flavour to this unusual soup.

2 teaspoons polyunsaturated margarine
1 large onion, chopped
270 g (9 oz) cauliflower, broken into florets
2 vegetable stock cubes, dissolved in 900 ml (1½ pints) boiling water
120 g (4 oz) low-fat soft cheese
60 g (2 oz) blue Stilton cheese, crumbled, or Danish Blue cheese
2 tablespoons snipped fresh chives
salt and freshly ground black pepper

1. Melt the margarine in a large saucepan and sauté the onion for about 3 minutes, until softened.
2. Add the cauliflower and vegetable stock to the saucepan and bring to the boil. Cover and cook over a very low heat for about 15 minutes, or until the cauliflower is tender.
3. Transfer to a liquidiser or food processor and blend for about 15 seconds. Reserve 2 tablespoons of the soft cheese and then add the remainder to the soup in the liquidiser. Add the blue cheese and half the chives. Blend for a few more seconds, until smooth. Return to the saucepan and reheat gently. Season to taste with salt and pepper.
4. Ladle the soup into warmed bowls and spoon a little reserved soft cheese on top of each portion. Sprinkle with the remaining chives and a little pepper. Serve at once.

Points per serving: 3
Total Points per recipe: 12

Creamy Autumn Vegetable Soup

Serves 4

Preparation and cooking time:
35 minutes
Calories per serving: 140

Freezing: recommended

Warming, nutritious and so easy to make, this delicious soup will welcome you in from the cold.

2 teaspoons polyunsaturated margarine
1 onion, chopped finely
1 carrot, chopped
180 g (6 oz) swede or turnip, diced
240 g (8 oz) potato, diced
1 vegetable stock cube, dissolved in 600 ml (1 pint) boiling water
1 tablespoon cornflour
300 ml (½ pint) skimmed milk
120 g (4 oz) low-fat natural fromage frais
salt and freshly ground black pepper
chopped fresh parsley, to garnish

1. Melt the margarine in a large saucepan and sauté the onion gently until softened, about 3 minutes.
2. Add the carrot, swede or turnip, potato and vegetable stock. Bring to the boil and then reduce the heat. Cook, covered, for 15–20 minutes, until the vegetables are tender.
3. Blend the cornflour with 2–3 tablespoons of the skimmed milk. Add the remaining milk to the saucepan, with the fromage frais. Stir in the blended cornflour. Heat gently, stirring constantly, until almost boiling and slightly thickened.
4. Season to taste with salt and pepper. Ladle into warmed soup bowls and serve at once, garnished with parsley.

Points per serving: 2
Total Points per recipe: 8

Lentil, Tomato and Red Pepper Soup

Serves 4

Preparation and cooking time:
45 minutes
Calories per serving: 110

Freezing: recommended

2 teaspoons olive or vegetable oil
1 onion, chopped
2 red peppers, de-seeded and chopped
1 tablespoon paprika
1 vegetable stock cube, dissolved in 600 ml (1 pint) boiling water
300 ml (½ pint) tomato juice
60 g (2 oz) red lentils
salt and freshly ground black pepper
To garnish:
2 tablespoons low-fat natural yogurt
chopped fresh coriander or parsley

1. Heat the oil in a large saucepan. Reserve a little chopped onion and red pepper and add the remainder to the saucepan. Sauté gently for about 5 minutes, until softened. Add the paprika and cook gently for 1 minute more.
2. Add the vegetable stock, tomato juice and lentils to the saucepan. Bring to the boil and then reduce the heat. Cover and cook over a very low heat for about 30 minutes, until the lentils are soft.
3. Transfer the soup to a liquidiser or food processor and blend for about 15 seconds, until smooth. Return to the saucepan and reheat gently. Season to taste with salt and pepper.
4. Ladle the soup into warmed bowls and spoon a little yogurt on to each portion. Scatter the reserved onion and pepper on top and sprinkle with coriander or parsley.

Points per serving: 1
Total Points per recipe: 4

Snacks

There are times when you really need a snack; sometimes you are genuinely hungry and at other times you just want something to nibble. Perhaps you are having a few friends around, or maybe you need something to tide you over to your main meal. Whatever the reason, you will find that these ideas fit the bill precisely, without ruining your good intentions!

Vegetable Crudités with Garlic and Herb Dip

Serves 4

Preparation time: 5 minutes
Calories per serving: 105

Freezing: not recommended

V if using vegetarian cheese

Just the thing for a quick and tasty snack, this dip makes raw vegetable sticks far more interesting! Use as many fresh herbs as you have but you can also just use one in this recipe.

210 g (7 oz) low-fat soft cheese with garlic
4 tablespoons low-fat natural yogurt
1 celery stick, chopped very finely
1 tablespoon chopped fresh herbs, e.g. chives, parsley, oregano or mint
1/2 teaspoon paprika
salt and freshly ground black pepper
To serve:
360 g (12 oz) raw vegetables, e.g. cucumber, spring onions, peppers, cauliflower, carrot, etc., cut in sticks

1. Beat together the soft cheese and yogurt, until smooth. Add the celery, herbs and paprika and mix well. Season with salt and pepper.
2. Tip the dip into a serving bowl and serve with the raw vegetables.

Cook's note:
If you can't find low-fat soft cheese with garlic, flavour plain soft cheese with 1 teaspoon of garlic purée or a small crushed garlic clove.

Points per serving: 1 1/2
Total Points per recipe: 6

Pink Salmon Pâté

Serves 4

Preparation time: 5 minutes
Calories per serving: 105

Freezing: not recommended

This easy pâté tastes great spread on crispbreads and toast or just served with salad – and it's all prepared in 5 minutes flat! When serving with crispbread, rolls, toast, pitta bread, or with a fresh salad, remember to count the extra Points.

210 g (7 oz) canned pink salmon, drained
2 celery sticks, chopped finely
2 spring onions, chopped finely
4 tablespoons low-calorie mayonnaise
1 tablespoon chopped fresh parsley or chives
2 teaspoons lemon juice or a few drops of light malt vinegar
salt and freshly ground black pepper

1. Tip the salmon into a mixing bowl and mash well with a fork. Add the celery, spring onions, mayonnaise, parsley or chives, and lemon juice or vinegar. Stir well to combine thoroughly. Season to taste with salt and pepper.
2. Cover and refrigerate the pâté until ready to use.

Cook's note:
The pâté will keep, covered and refrigerated, for 4–5 days.

Points per serving: 2 1/2
Total Points per recipe: 10

Fresh Salad Pitta

Serves 4

Preparation time: 10 minutes
Calories per serving: 260

Freezing: not recommended

V if using free-range eggs

Fresh salad, packed into warm pitta bread and drizzled with a light mint or coriander dressing. Delicious!

2 tablespoons low-calorie mayonnaise
4 tablespoons low-fat natural yogurt
1 tablespoon chopped fresh mint or coriander (optional)
4 standard pitta breads
120 g (4 oz) mixed lettuce leaves, shredded
4 spring onions, chopped finely
5 cm (2-inch) piece of cucumber, chopped
12 cherry tomatoes, halved
2 eggs, hard-boiled and sliced
salt and freshly ground black pepper

1. Mix the mayonnaise and yogurt together and add the mint or coriander (if using).
2. Warm the pitta breads. Split and fill with lettuce, spring onions, cucumber, tomatoes and eggs. Season with salt and pepper. Spoon an equal amount of dressing into each pitta and serve at once.

Points per serving: 3¹/₂
Total Points per recipe: 14

Creamy Cheese, Carrot and Cucumber Bagels

Serves 4

Preparation time: **10 minutes**
Calories per serving: **225**

Freezing: not recommended

V if using vegetarian cheese

Soft, chewy bagels make a deliciously different snack; just half a medium-sized one will be enough to keep you going!

2 bagels, halved horizontally
120 g (4 oz) low-fat soft cheese
1 tablespoon skimmed milk
30 g (1 oz) sultanas or raisins
5 cm (2-inch) piece of cucumber, chopped finely
60 g (2 oz) double Gloucester or Cheddar cheese, grated
1 small carrot, grated
salt and freshly ground black pepper

1. Lightly toast the bagels on their cut surfaces.
2. Meanwhile, mix together the soft cheese, milk, sultanas or raisins, cucumber and grated cheese. Season with salt and pepper. Spread over the warm bagels.
3. Sprinkle with grated carrot and serve at once.

Points per serving: 4¹/₂
Total Points per recipe: 18

Tasty Italian Bread Bites

Serves 4

Preparation and cooking time:
15 minutes
Calories per serving: 285

Freezing: not recommended

V if using vegetarian mozzarella

You can make these tasty morsels with Italian ciabatta bread, which is available from most supermarkets, or you can use french bread.

2 teaspoons olive oil
1 small red onion or 4 spring onions, chopped finely
60 g (2 oz) button mushrooms, sliced
1 teaspoon dried mixed Italian herbs
4 teaspoons sun-dried tomato paste or tomato purée
2 teaspoons garlic purée (optional)
8 × 30 g (1 oz) slices of Italian ciabatta or french bread
4 large tomatoes, sliced thinly
120 g (4 oz) mozzarella cheese, grated
salt and freshly ground black pepper

1. Preheat the oven to Gas Mark 6/200°C/400°F.
2. Heat the oil in a small saucepan and sauté the onion or spring onions for 2 minutes, until softened. Add the mushrooms and herbs and cook for 1 minute more.
3. Mix the tomato paste or purée with the garlic purée, if using. Spread evenly over the slices of bread. Place the pieces of bread on a baking sheet and divide the mushroom mixture between them. Season with salt and pepper. Arrange the sliced tomatoes on top and sprinkle with mozzarella cheese.
4. Bake in the oven for 10–12 minutes, until crisp and golden. Serve at once.

Cook's note:
Buy ready-grated mozzarella cheese for convenience (you'll find that the blocks are tricky to grate).

Points per serving: 5
Total Points per recipe: 20

Salads

You'll enjoy the great taste of fresh flavours in these salads. Each one is full of interesting textures and glorious colours. After all, food should be about great sensations: it should be a feast for the eyes as well as satisfying your appetite. Remember to make the best use of seasonal salad ingredients – including vegetables and fruit – and use them while they are at their freshest. That way you will get more of their delicious flavours and the nutritive value will be at its best.

Fruity Roast Chicken Salad

Serves 4

Preparation time: 10 minutes
Calories per serving: 175

Freezing: not recommended

Chicken tastes especially good with fruity flavours. Try it in this salad with crunchy apples and seedless grapes.

2 tablespoons lemon juice
1 medium-size green eating apple, cored and chopped
1 medium-size red eating apple, cored and chopped
60 g (2 oz) red or green seedless grapes, halved
30 g (1 oz) sultanas
4 celery sticks, chopped
240 g (8 oz) skinless roast chicken, chopped
2 teaspoons snipped fresh chives
4 tablespoons low-fat natural yogurt
salt and freshly ground black pepper
To serve:
iceberg lettuce leaves
2 teaspoons pine kernels, toasted (optional)
chive flowers (optional)

1. Put the lemon juice in a large bowl and add the apples, tossing to coat. Add the grapes, sultanas, celery, chicken, chives and yogurt. Season with salt and pepper.
2. Arrange the lettuce on serving plates and spoon the salad on top. Sprinkle with the pine kernels (if using) and garnish with chive flowers (if using).

Points per serving: 3¹/₂
Total Points per recipe: 14

Spinach, Avocado and Turkey Salad

Serves 4

Preparation and cooking time: 10 minutes
Calories per serving: 110

Freezing: not recommended

A little ripe avocado tastes wonderful in this fresh spinach salad. Delicious snippets of grilled turkey rasher finish it off.

120 g (4 oz) low-fat turkey rashers
2 tablespoons lemon juice
1 tablespoon smoky barbecue sauce
240 g (8 oz) young spinach leaves
¹/₂ medium-size avocado
4 tablespoons low-fat natural yogurt
2 teaspoons chopped fresh herbs, e.g. chives, parsley, oregano, etc.
30 g (1 oz) garlic and herb croûtons
salt and freshly ground black pepper

1. Preheat the grill. Lay the turkey rashers on the grill pan. Mix a tablespoon of lemon juice with the barbecue sauce and brush over the rashers. Grill for about 4 minutes, without turning, until browned. Allow to cool slightly.
2. Meanwhile, rinse the spinach leaves and divide between four serving bowls. Peel and chop the avocado and toss it in the remaining lemon juice, to prevent it from going brown. Divide the avocado flesh between the salads.
3. Snip the turkey rashers into fine shreds and sprinkle over the leaves. Mix the yogurt with the herbs and use to dress the salads. Sprinkle the croûtons on top and season with salt and pepper.

Points per serving: 2
Total Points per recipe: 8

Continental Salad

Serves 4

Preparation time: 10 minutes
Calories per serving: 235

Freezing: not recommended

This tasty main-course salad can be assembled in minutes.

1 iceberg lettuce, shredded
1 radicchio head, torn in pieces
120 g (4 oz) wafer-thin German ham, torn in strips
120 g (4 oz) Edam or Emmenthal cheese, sliced finely
10 cm (4-inch) piece of cucumber, sliced
120 g (4 oz) cherry tomatoes, halved
4 teaspoons olive oil
2 tablespoons red-wine or white-wine vinegar
1 teaspoon Dijon mustard
30 g (1 oz) garlic croûtons
salt and freshly ground black pepper

1. Arrange the iceberg and radicchio on four serving plates.
2. Divide the ham and cheese equally between the portions. Arrange the cucumber and cherry tomatoes on top.
3. To make the dressing, whisk the olive oil, vinegar and mustard together. Season with salt and pepper and pour over the salads. Sprinkle the garlic croûtons on top and serve.

Cook's note:
Look out for packets of ready-made croûtons, available from supermarkets. They are usually situated near to the soups and come in some excellent flavours, including garlic, and garlic and herb.

Points per serving: 5
Total Points per recipe: 20

Chick-pea and Tuna Salad

v. good, especially the next day.
? needs more dressing.

Serves 4

Preparation time: 10 minutes
Calories per serving: 220

Freezing: not recommended

Chick-peas taste very good with tuna, in a lemon juice, garlic and fresh-herb dressing.

For the dressing:
1 garlic clove, crushed
1 tablespoon chopped fresh parsley
finely grated zest of 1 lemon
4 tablespoons lemon juice
1 tablespoon olive oil
salt and freshly ground black pepper

For the salad:
420 g (14 oz) canned tuna fish in brine, drained
450 g (15 oz) canned chick-peas, rinsed and drained
1 red onion, sliced thinly
5 cm (2-inch) piece of cucumber, chopped finely
2 tomatoes, chopped
mixed lettuce leaves, to serve
fresh parsley sprigs, to garnish

1. For the dressing, mix together the garlic, parsley, lemon zest and lemon juice, in a small jug. Add the olive oil and seasoning, stirring well.
2. Flake the tuna fish into chunks and add to the chick-peas, with the red onion, cucumber and tomatoes. Add the dressing and toss the ingredients together gently.
3. Arrange the lettuce leaves on four plates. Divide the tuna salad between each serving. Garnish with parsley sprigs and serve at once.

Points per serving: 4
Total Points per recipe: 16

Oriental Prawn Salad

Serves 4

Preparation and cooking time:
12 minutes
Calories per serving: 120

Freezing: not recommended

Coat prawns in sesame seeds, stir-fry until crisp and then serve hot in this colourful salad.

1 bag of mixed salad leaves or
   1 medium lettuce
4 celery sticks, sliced
1 small yellow or green pepper,
   de-seeded and chopped
1 small red onion, sliced finely
1 bunch of radishes
240 g (8 oz) large prawns,
   defrosted if frozen
1 tablespoon sesame seeds
1 tablespoon sesame or
   vegetable oil
4 teaspoons white wine vinegar
salt and freshly ground black
   pepper

1. Arrange the salad leaves on four serving plates, with the celery, pepper, onion and radishes.
2. Roll the prawns in the sesame seeds. Heat the oil in a frying-pan and add the prawns. Stir-fry over a high heat for about a minute, until crisp. Drain on kitchen paper and then divide between the salads.
3. Season the salads with vinegar, salt and pepper and serve at once.

Cook's note:
Use cooked chicken breast instead of prawns, for a change. Points per serving will be the same.

Points per serving: 2
Total Points per recipe: 8

Vegetable Salad with Fresh Herb Dressing

Serves 4

Preparation and cooking time:
15 minutes
Calories per serving: 100

Freezing: not recommended

Steam lots of colourful summer vegetables and then dress them with a light vinaigrette, flavoured with garden-fresh herbs, to make a spectacular salad.

180 g (6 oz) new carrots
180 g (6 oz) baby sweetcorn, halved lengthways
120 g (4 oz) mangetout or green beans
2 celery sticks, sliced
12 radishes, halved
180 g (6 oz) small asparagus spears
For the dressing:
4 teaspoons olive oil
1/2 teaspoon finely grated lemon zest
4 teaspoons lemon juice
4 teaspoons white wine vinegar
2 teaspoons chopped fresh thyme or dill
2 teaspoons chopped fresh chives or parsley
salt and freshly ground black pepper
1 teaspoon sesame seeds, lightly toasted, to garnish

1. Steam the carrots, baby corn, mangetout or green beans, celery, radishes and asparagus over gently boiling water, until just tender, about 5 minutes. It is important that the vegetables retain a slightly crunchy texture.
2. Meanwhile make the dressing. Mix the oil with the lemon zest, lemon juice and vinegar. Stir in the herbs and then season with salt and pepper.
3. When the vegetables are cooked, drain well and then toss in the dressing. Allow to cool and then transfer them to four individual serving plates. Sprinkle with the toasted sesame seeds and serve immediately.

Points per serving: 1 1/2
Total Points per recipe: 6

Mediterranean Salad

Serves 4

Preparation and cooking time:
15 minutes
Calories per serving: 100

Freezing: not recommended

 if using vegetarian feta

Choose a few inspired ingredients to make this sunny salad.

120 g (4 oz) shelled broad beans
finely grated zest of 1/2 lemon
4 teaspoons olive oil
4 teaspoons red wine vinegar
1 tablespoon chopped fresh oregano or basil
1 bunch of spring onions, chopped finely
7.5 cm (3-inch) piece of cucumber, sliced
4 plum tomatoes, quartered
1 Cos or Romaine lettuce, shredded roughly
120 g (4 oz) feta cheese, cut into small cubes
salt and freshly ground black pepper

1. Cook the broad beans in a small amount of lightly salted water, until just tender. Drain well and then transfer to a salad bowl. Add the lemon zest, oil, vinegar, herbs and spring onions. Stir well and leave to cool.
2. Add the cucumber, tomatoes, lettuce and cheese. Season lightly with salt and plenty of pepper.
3. To serve, toss all the salad ingredients together well, to distribute the dressing evenly over all the ingredients.

Cook's note:
Adding the dressing to the broad beans while they are still warm means that they absorb its flavour.

Points per serving: 4
Total Points per recipe: 16

Crisp Bacon and Egg Salad

Serves 4

Preparation and cooking time:
20 minutes
Calories per serving: 225

Freezing: not recommended

Crisp bacon bits, hard-boiled eggs and strips of roasted red pepper make up this colourful salad, with its tantalising flavours and textures.

2 red peppers, halved and de-seeded
60 g (2 oz) lean back bacon
4 eggs, hard-boiled
1 large bag of mixed lettuce leaves
4 tomatoes, sliced
60 g (2 oz) croûtons
For the dressing:
4 tablespoons low-fat natural yogurt
1 tablespoon chopped fresh parsley
1 teaspoon finely grated lemon zest
salt and freshly ground black pepper

1. Preheat the grill. Place the peppers on the grill rack, skin-side up. Grill until the skin becomes blackened and blistered. Remove from the heat, cover with a damp cloth and leave to cool. Peel off and discard the skins. Cut the peppers into strips.
2. Meanwhile, grill the bacon until it's very crisp. Drain on kitchen paper and snip into tiny pieces. Shell the hard-boiled eggs and cut them in half.
3. Arrange the lettuce on four plates, with the tomatoes. Sprinkle with the crisp bacon and arrange the eggs on top. Scatter an equal amount of croûtons over each portion.
4. To make the dressing, mix together the yogurt, parsley and lemon zest. Season with salt and pepper. Drizzle over the salad.

Cook's note:
Canned, drained pimientos can be used as an alternative to fresh red peppers; or look out for pickled pepper strips, which can be used instead.

Points per serving: 3
Total Points per recipe: 12

Seafood

In this country we are so lucky to have a good choice of fresh fish. It's also useful to have frozen and canned fish as standbys: you never know when you are going to be called upon to create something tasty. In this chapter, you will find interesting recipes to make the most of all three, depending on what you have available. You can always consult this chapter if you run out of ideas – it's sure to come up with the goods!

Prawn and Scallop Skewers

Serves 4

Preparation and cooking time:
13 minutes
Calories per serving: 130

Freezing: not recommended

Thread some juicy prawns and tiny scallops on to skewers, brush them with lemony herb baste and then grill or barbecue them to perfection.

2 lemons
2 tablespoons chopped fresh
   herbs, e.g. parsley, chives,
   dill, marjoram, etc.
2 teaspoons olive oil
360 g (12 oz) large frozen
   prawns, defrosted
120 g (4 oz) small scallops,
   defrosted
16 cherry tomatoes
salt and freshly ground black
   pepper
mixed salad leaves, to serve

1. Cut one of the lemons into thick slices and then cut each slice into four. Finely grate the rind and squeeze the juice from the remaining lemon and mix with the herbs and oil. Season with salt and pepper.
2. Thread the prawns, scallops, cherry tomatoes and lemon pieces on skewers.
3. Preheat the grill or barbecue and divide the salad leaves between four plates. Place the kebabs on the grill rack and brush with the lemon and herb baste. Grill or barbecue for about 3 minutes, turning and basting occasionally. Put the kebabs on the plates and serve at once.

Points per serving: 2¹/₂
Total Points per recipe: 10

Quick Noodles with Crab and Coriander

Serves 4

Preparation and cooking time:
20 minutes
Calories per serving: 240

Freezing: not recommended

Rice noodles are very handy, as they only take moments to cook. Served with crab and fresh coriander, they make a speedy, satisfying meal.

180 g (6 oz) rice noodles
1 tablespoon sesame or
   vegetable oil
1 garlic clove, crushed
6 shallots, sliced
1 red pepper, de-seeded and
   sliced
240 g (8 oz) canned crabmeat,
   drained and flaked roughly
¹/₂ teaspoon finely grated fresh
   root ginger
1 tablespoon chopped fresh
   coriander
1 tablespoon teriyaki or soy
   sauce
salt and freshly ground black
   pepper

1. Soak the noodles in boiling water for about 6 minutes, according to the packet instructions.
2. Meanwhile, heat the oil in a wok or large frying-pan and stir-fry the garlic, shallots and red pepper for 2–3 minutes.
3. Add the crabmeat, ginger, coriander and teriyaki or soy sauce, and stir-fry for 2 minutes more. Season and serve with the drained noodles.

Points per serving: 3¹/₂
Total Points per recipe: 14

Italian Fish Sauté

Serves 4

Preparation and cooking time:
20 minutes
Calories per serving: 205

Freezing: not recommended

Hake is a very popular fish
in Mediterranean climates.
It tastes superb sautéed with
red onion, garlic, tomatoes,
lemon juice and oregano.
Serve with fresh vegetables
or a salad.

2 tablespoons plain flour
2 teaspoons finely grated
   lemon zest
540 g (1 lb 2 oz) hake, cod or
   haddock (or any firm white
   fish), skinned and boned
2 tablespoons olive oil
1–2 garlic cloves, crushed
1 red onion, sliced
4 tomatoes, skinned, de-seeded
   and chopped
2 tablespoons lemon juice
2 teaspoons capers (optional)
1 tablespoon chopped fresh
   oregano
salt and freshly ground black
   pepper

1. Sprinkle the flour on to a plate, add the lemon zest and season
with salt and pepper. Cut the fish into large chunks and coat the
chunks in the flour mixture.
2. Heat the oil in a frying-pan and sauté the garlic and onion until
softened, about 3 minutes. Add the fish and sauté for 2–3 more
minutes, and then add the tomatoes, lemon juice, capers (if using)
and oregano. Cook, stirring gently, until the fish is opaque, about
2 more minutes.
3. Season with salt and pepper and serve at once.

Cook's notes:
Skin tomatoes by putting them into a heatproof bowl and covering
them with boiling water. Leave for a minute and then slip off their
skins. To save time, use a small (210 g/7 oz) can of chopped
tomatoes instead.

Points per serving: 3½
Total Points per recipe: 14

Tiger Prawns in Thai Curry Sauce

Serves 4

Preparation and cooking time:
22 minutes
Calories per serving: 390

Freezing: not recommended

Assemble all your ingredients
and then cook this exciting
Thai recipe in a flash!

180 g (6 oz) long-grain rice
1 tablespoon sesame or
   vegetable oil
6 spring onions, sliced
½ teaspoon finely grated fresh
   root ginger
finely grated zest of 1 lemon
240 ml (8 fl oz) canned
   coconut milk
2 tablespoons Thai red or
   green curry paste
1 tablespoon Thai fish sauce or
   light soy sauce
480 g (1 lb) shelled tiger
   prawns or king prawns,
   defrosted if frozen
1 tablespoon chopped fresh
   coriander or parsley
fresh coriander or parsley
   sprigs, to garnish

1. Cook the rice in plenty of boiling, lightly salted water for about
12 minutes, until tender.
2. Heat the oil in a frying-pan and sauté the spring onions until
softened, about 2 minutes. Add the ginger and lemon zest, with the
coconut milk, curry paste and fish sauce or soy sauce. Heat until
almost boiling.
3. Add the prawns to the frying-pan, with the chopped coriander or
parsley and cook gently for 3 minutes.
4. Serve the prawns with the drained, cooked rice. Spoon over the
sauce and garnish with sprigs of fresh coriander or parsley.

Cook's note:
Remember that you can use the stems of fresh coriander as well as
the leaves; just chop them finely first.

Points per serving: 10
Total Points per recipe: 40

Tuna and Fresh Herb Frittata

Serves 4

Preparation and cooking time:
25 minutes
Calories per serving: 240

Freezing: not recommended

**Canned tuna is so versatile!
Add it to a frittata for a quick,
tasty meal.**

1 tablespoon olive oil
360 g (12 oz) cooked potatoes,
    cubed
1 small onion, sliced finely
1 courgette, chopped finely
210 g (7 oz) canned tuna in
    brine, flaked roughly
3 eggs
1 tablespoon skimmed milk
30 g (1 oz) Cheddar cheese,
    grated
salt and freshly ground black
    pepper
chopped fresh herbs, to garnish

1. Heat the oil in a medium frying-pan and sauté the potatoes,
until browned. Add the onion and courgette and sauté for 2–3 more
minutes. Scatter the flaked tuna over the surface.
2. Beat the eggs and milk together and season with salt and pepper.
Add to the pan and cook over a low heat until set. Sprinkle the
cheese on top and grill until lightly browned. Cut into wedges and
serve at once, sprinkled with herbs.

Cook's note:
Use canned crabmeat as an alternative to tuna.

Points per serving: 4¹/₂
Total Points per recipe: 18

Poached Trout with Coriander Mayonnaise

Serves 4

Preparation and cooking time:
30 minutes
Calories per serving: 360

Freezing: not recommended

**The delicate flavour of
poached fresh trout tastes
wonderful with this excellent
coriander mayonnaise.**

4 × 150 g (5 oz) trout fillets
1 teaspoon vinegar
3 tablespoons low-calorie
    mayonnaise
2 tablespoons low-fat natural
    yogurt
1 tablespoon chopped fresh
    coriander
720 g (1¹/₂ lb) baby new
    potatoes
360 g (12 oz) dwarf green beans
    or young asparagus spears
salt and freshly ground black
    pepper

1. Place the trout fillets in a large shallow pan that has a lid. Add
300 ml (¹/₂ pint) of cold water and the vinegar. Cover and bring the
water to the boil; then turn off the heat. Keep the saucepan covered
and allow the fish to cool.
2. Mix together the mayonnaise, yogurt and coriander. Season with
salt and pepper. Refrigerate until required.
3. Cook the potatoes and beans or asparagus until just tender.
4. Serve the poached trout topped with the coriander mayonnaise
and accompanied by the vegetables.

Cook's note:
Chopped fresh dill or marjoram also tastes excellent with fish, so
try them as alternatives to coriander.

Points per serving: 5
Total Points per recipe: 20

Friday Fish Pie

Serves 4

Preparation and cooking time:
40 minutes
Calories per serving: 490

Freezing: not recommended

**Enjoy the tradition of eating
fish on Friday by making this
delicious fish pie.**

450 ml (¾ pint) skimmed milk
1 teaspoon mixed dried Italian
   herbs
30 g (1 oz) polyunsaturated
   margarine
60 g (2 oz) plain flour
60 g (2 oz) shelled prawns,
   defrosted if frozen
420 g (14 oz) skinless, boneless
   cod or haddock, cubed
720 g (1½ lb) cooked potatoes,
   sliced
150 ml (5 fl oz) low-fat natural
   yogurt
1 egg
60 g (2 oz) mature Cheddar
   cheese, grated
salt and freshly ground black
   pepper

1. Preheat the oven to Gas Mark 5/190°C/375°F.
2. Put the milk, dried herbs, margarine and flour into a saucepan.
Heat, stirring constantly with a small wire whisk, until thickened
and smooth. Add the prawns and season with salt and pepper.
3. Place the fish in the base of a 1.2-litre (2-pint) baking dish. Pour
over the sauce. Arrange the sliced potatoes neatly over the surface.
4. Beat together the yogurt and egg and then stir in the grated
cheese. Season with salt and pepper and spread over the surface
of the potatoes. Bake in the oven for 25–30 minutes, until golden
brown.

Cook's notes:
Use smoked cod or haddock for a more robust flavour and, if you
wish, leave out the prawns.

Points per serving: 8½
Total Points per recipe: 34

Chicken and Turkey

There is no doubt that a whole chapter devoted to chicken and turkey is well worthwhile: both are readily available, economical and very versatile. What's more, they are very low in fat, making them ideal choices for anyone concerned with losing weight and maintaining a healthy diet. The recipes here are full of fabulous flavours, making a world of difference to your everyday eating!

Parmesan Chicken with Tomatoes and Courgettes

Serves 4

Preparation and cooking time:
25 minutes
Calories per serving: 300

Freezing: not recommended

Chicken cooks brilliantly in the microwave, and tastes especially good with this tasty breadcrumb, herb and parmesan cheese coating. You can also cook it in a conventional oven if you prefer.

30 g (1 oz) plain flour
4 × 150 g (5 oz) skinless, boneless chicken breasts
30 g (1 oz) dried breadcrumbs
30 g (1 oz) parmesan cheese, grated finely
1 teaspoon dried mixed Italian herbs
1 egg, beaten
4 teaspoons olive oil
1 onion, chopped
4 tomatoes, quartered
1 courgette, sliced
1 tablespoon chopped fresh basil (optional)
salt and freshly ground black pepper

1. Sprinkle the flour on to a plate and season it with salt and pepper. Rinse the chicken breasts and coat them with the seasoned flour. Mix together the breadcrumbs, cheese and dried herbs.
2. Dip each chicken breast into the beaten egg and then coat with the breadcrumb mixture. Lay the chicken in a shallow, microwave-safe dish. In microwave ovens, foods placed around the edge of the oven cook more quickly than foods placed in the center. So arrange the thicker parts of the chicken breast towards the edge of the dish and the thinner parts to the middle. Cover loosely with greaseproof paper.
3. Microwave on HIGH for 6–8 minutes, rearranging the chicken halfway through the cooking time. Allow to stand while you cook the vegetables.
4. Put the oil into a microwave-safe bowl and add the onion. Microwave on HIGH for 4 minutes, stirring once after 2 minutes. Add the tomatoes, courgette and basil (if using) and microwave on HIGH for a further 2–3 minutes, stirring once. Season with salt and pepper. Serve the chicken breasts accompanied by the vegetables.

Cook's notes:
Timings may vary, according to the power of your microwave; check your manufacturer's handbook for further guidance. For conventional cooking, preheat the oven to Gas Mark 6/200°C/400°F. Roast the coated chicken breasts for 25–30 minutes or until the juices run clear when the thickest part is pierced with a sharp knife. Meanwhile, lightly sauté the onion for 3 minutes. Then add the tomatoes, courgettes and basil, cooking over a very low heat for 10 minutes.

Points per serving: 6
Total Points per recipe: 24

Middle Eastern Turkey

Serves 4

Preparation and cooking time:
35 minutes
Calories per serving: 285

Freezing: not recommended

This Middle-Eastern style turkey dish is made in a flash and it's full of wonderful flavours!

1 tablespoon vegetable oil
1 large onion, chopped
480 g (1 lb) fresh turkey steaks, cubed
1 tablespoon chopped fresh mint or coriander, plus extra to garnish, or 1 teaspoon dried
finely grated zest and juice of 1 medium-size orange
1/2 teaspoon ground cinnamon
1/2 teaspoon cumin seeds or ground cumin
450 g (15 oz) canned chick-peas, rinsed and drained
30 g (1 oz) sultanas
1 tablespoon cornflour
4 tablespoons low-fat natural yogurt
salt and freshly ground black pepper

1. Heat the oil in a frying-pan and sauté the onion until softened, about 3 minutes. Add the turkey and cook for 5 more minutes, until sealed and browned on the outside.
2. Stir in the mint or coriander, orange zest and juice, cinnamon, cumin, chick-peas and sultanas. Cover and cook over a low heat for 20 minutes.
3. Blend the cornflour with a little cold water and then mix with the yogurt. Stir into the turkey and heat until thickened. Cook gently for 2 more minutes. Season to taste with salt and pepper and serve, sprinkled with extra chopped mint or coriander.

Cook's notes:
Chicken may be used instead of turkey and the Points will be the same. Try using ground ginger instead of cumin, for a change.

Points per serving: 6
Total Points per recipe: 24

Turkey Jambalaya

Serves 4

Preparation and cooking time:
35 minutes
Calories per serving: 195

Freezing: recommended

A plateful of this delicious spicy turkey and rice dish will soon satisfy your hunger!

1 tablespoon vegetable oil
360 g (12 oz) skinless, boneless turkey steak, cubed
1 onion, chopped finely
2 garlic cloves, crushed
2 celery sticks, chopped
1 small green pepper, de-seeded and chopped
120 g (4 oz) button mushrooms
4 tomatoes, chopped
360 g (12 oz) cooked long-grain rice
1 teaspoon dried thyme
2 teaspoons Cajun seasoning or paprika
1/2 teaspoon mild chilli powder
salt and freshly ground black pepper

1. Heat the oil in a frying-pan and sauté the turkey until browned, about 5 minutes. Add the onion and cook until softened, 3–4 minutes more.
2. Add the garlic, celery, green pepper, mushrooms and tomatoes and continue to cook for 5 more minutes.
3. Stir in the cooked rice, thyme, Cajun seasoning or paprika and chilli powder. Cook for 3–4 minutes more, stirring constantly, until heated through. Check the seasoning, adding salt and pepper and a little more chilli powder if required. Spoon on to warm plates and serve at once.

Cook's notes:
If you're not keen on spicy foods, just leave out the Cajun seasoning or paprika and chilli powder and add about a tablespoon of chopped fresh basil.

Points per serving: 4 1/2
Total Points per recipe: 18

Sweetcorn Pancakes with Roast Chicken and Spicy Salsa

Serves 4

Preparation and cooking time:
35 minutes
Calories per serving: 305

Freezing: not recommended

Small sweetcorn pancakes are topped here with strips of roast chicken and a spoonful of spicy sauce.

For the pancakes:
120 g (4 oz) plain flour
pinch of salt
1 large egg, beaten
210 ml (7 fl oz) skimmed milk
90 g (3 oz) canned or frozen
    sweetcorn, defrosted
2 teaspoons vegetable oil

For the topping:
2 teaspoons vegetable oil
240 g (8 oz) skinless, boneless
    cooked chicken, sliced
1 teaspoon Cajun seasoning or
    1/2 teaspoon mild chilli
    powder
shredded lettuce
4 spring onions, chopped finely
1 tomato, chopped finely
5 cm (2–inch) piece of
    cucumber, chopped finely
4 tablespoons tomato juice
a few drops of Tabasco sauce
    (optional)
salt and freshly ground black
    pepper
chopped fresh coriander or
    parsley, to garnish

1. To make the batter, sift the flour and salt into a large mixing bowl. Add the egg and milk and whisk together to make a smooth batter. Stir in the sweetcorn.
2. Heat a heavy-based frying-pan and add a few drops of oil. Spoon one quarter of the batter into the pan and cook over a medium-high heat, until set, about 2 minutes. Turn over and cook the other side. Make three more pancakes with the remaining batter, keeping them in a warm place as they are cooked.
3. For the topping, heat the oil in a frying-pan and sauté the chicken for 2–3 minutes, adding the Cajun seasoning or chilli powder. Divide between the pancakes and top with shredded lettuce.
4. Mix together the spring onions, tomato, cucumber and tomato juice. Season with a few drops of Tabasco sauce, if you like, and some salt and pepper. Spoon a little on top of each pancake and garnish with fresh coriander or parsley.

Points per serving: 41/2
Total Points per recipe: 18

Chicken Breasts with Spicy Baste

Serves 4

Preparation and cooking time:
35 minutes
Calories per serving: 155

Freezing: not recommended

Marinate chicken breasts in a spicy lime-juice mixture, grill or barbecue them and then serve them with a good squeeze of lime juice.

2 teaspoons olive oil
1 tablespoon paprika
1/2 teaspoon cumin seeds or
    ground cumin
2 teaspoons finely grated fresh
    root ginger
3 tablespoons lime juice
1 tablespoon chopped fresh
    thyme or mint
4 × 120 g (4 oz) skinless,
    boneless chicken breasts
fresh thyme or mint sprigs
salt and freshly ground black
    pepper
lime wedges, to garnish

1. In a shallow bowl, mix together the olive oil, paprika, cumin, ginger, lime juice and chopped herbs. Season with salt and pepper.
2. Lay the chicken breasts in the lime juice mixture. Cover, refrigerate and allow to marinate for 10 minutes.
3. Grill or barbecue the chicken for about 15 minutes, turning once and basting with the marinade, until tender. When tested with a fork, the juices should run clear.
4. Serve the chicken garnished with fresh thyme or mint sprigs and lime wedges.

Cook's notes:
If you have time to marinate the chicken for longer (about an hour), you'll get more of the spicy flavour.

Points per serving: 3
Total Points per recipe: 12

Coriander Turkey

Serves 4

Preparation and cooking time:
40 minutes
Calories per serving: 205

Freezing: recommended

Fresh coriander has a delicious flavour. Make sure that you use the stems as well as the leaves.

2 tablespoons olive or vegetable oil
180 g (6 oz) shallots, sliced
480 g (1 lb) skinless, boneless turkey breasts, cubed
1 chicken stock cube, dissolved in 300 ml (½ pint) boiling water
180 g (6 oz) mushrooms, sliced
2 tablespoons chopped fresh coriander
1 tablespoon cornflour
salt and freshly ground black pepper
fresh coriander leaves, to garnish

1. Heat the oil in a large frying-pan, add the shallots and sauté them for 2–3 minutes. Add the turkey and sauté until browned, about 5 minutes.
2. Add the chicken stock to the frying-pan, with the mushrooms and coriander. Bring to the boil, cover and reduce the heat. Cook over a gentle heat for 15 minutes, until the turkey is tender.
3. Blend the cornflour with 2–3 tablespoons of cold water. Add to the frying-pan, stirring until blended and thickened. Cover and cook for 2 more minutes. Season with salt and pepper and serve, garnished with fresh coriander leaves.

Cook's notes:
Use a large onion instead of the shallots, if you prefer. For a change, substitute oregano for the coriander.
To store coriander frozen, put 1 teaspoon of chopped coriander into each compartment of an ice-cube tray and top up each one with water. 1 tablespoon = 3 ice-cubes.

Points per serving: 4
Total Points per recipe: 16

Chicken Breasts with Rosemary and Red Wine

Serves 4

Preparation and cooking time:
40 minutes
Calories per serving: 250

Freezing: recommended

Lean chicken breasts take on an Italian flavour in this quick-and-easy recipe. Serve with pasta or potatoes but don't forget to count the extra Points.

1 tablespoon olive or vegetable oil
1 garlic clove, crushed
2 red onions, sliced   +
2 celery sticks, sliced +
4 × 120 g (4 oz) skinless, boneless chicken breasts
120 ml (4 fl oz) red wine
1 chicken stock cube, dissolved in 150 ml (¼ pint) boiling water
10 small pitted black olives, halved
~~30 g (1 oz) sultanas~~
2 teaspoons capers (optional)
2 fresh rosemary sprigs
2 fresh thyme sprigs
1 tablespoon cornflour, blended with a little water
salt and freshly ground black pepper

1. Heat the oil in a flameproof casserole dish or saucepan and sauté the garlic, onions and celery for 2–3 minutes.
2. Add the chicken breasts to the casserole and cook for 2–3 minutes more, turning once, to brown them.
3. Pour in the wine and stock and add the olives, sultanas, capers (if using), rosemary and thyme. Season with salt and pepper. Bring to the boil, cover and reduce the heat. Cook for 20–25 minutes, until the chicken is tender.
4. Add the blended cornflour, stirring until thickened, and cook gently for 1 minute. Serve the chicken at once.

Points per serving: 5
Total Points per recipe: 20

Meat

Look at this chapter for inspiring, quick-and-easy meat dishes. Some of them are perfect for entertaining – such as the Chinese Pork and Noodle Stir-Fry – and some are ideal for family meals in moments; try Pasta with Smoked Ham and Tomato Sauce, for instance. There's even a lamb recipe for barbecuing and a garlicky bubble and squeak to make a tasty meal from leftovers. Choose whatever takes your fancy – you will surely find something here that appeals.

Grilled Lamb Steaks with Garlic and Rosemary Baste

Serves 4

Preparation and cooking time: 15 minutes
Calories per serving: 160

Freezing: not recommended

Lean lamb steaks can be cooked in minutes and they taste great when basted with this delicious garlicky and herby paste. Serve with a fresh green salad and sliced tomatoes or with fresh vegetables. Remember that adding a dressing will add extra Points.

4 × 120 g (4 oz) lean lamb steaks
2 garlic cloves, crushed
2 tablespoons lemon juice
1 teaspoon Dijon mustard
1 tablespoon light soy sauce
1 tablespoon chopped fresh rosemary or 2 teaspoons dried
salt and freshly ground black pepper

1. Preheat the grill.
2. Place the lamb steaks on the grill rack. Mix together the garlic, lemon juice, mustard and soy sauce. Add the rosemary and season with salt and pepper. Brush over the lamb.
3. Grill the lamb steaks for about 5 minutes. Turn them over and brush the other side with the baste. Cook for a further 5 minutes, or until cooked to your liking.

Points per serving: 4¹/₂
Total Points per recipe: 18

Lamb and Vegetable Stir-Fry

Serves 4

Preparation and cooking time: 22 minutes
Calories per serving: 185

Freezing: not recommended

Lean leg of lamb tastes excellent in this quick and easy stir-fry.

1 lamb or vegetable stock cube, dissolved in 150 ml (¹/₄ pint) hot water
1 tablespoon soy sauce or teriyaki marinade
1 tablespoon dark muscovado sugar
1 teaspoon grated fresh root ginger
1 tablespoon cornflour
1 tablespoon sesame or vegetable oil
360 g (12 oz) lean leg of lamb, sliced finely
1 bunch of spring onions, sliced
90 g (3 oz) mangetout
120 g (4 oz) broccoli, broken in small florets
1 red pepper, de-seeded and sliced
1 carrot, sliced thinly
salt and freshly ground black pepper

1. Mix together the stock, soy sauce or teriyaki marinade, sugar, ginger and cornflour. Season with a little salt and pepper.
2. Heat the oil in a wok or large frying-pan and add the lamb. Cook over a high heat, stirring constantly, for 4–5 minutes.
3. Add all the vegetables and continue to stir-fry for a further 4–5 minutes. Stir in the stock mixture and cook for about 2 minutes, until thickened. Serve at once.

Cook's notes:
Vary the vegetables according to the season or your preferences. Try mushrooms, green beans, celery, cauliflower and sugar-snap peas as alternatives.

Points per serving: 4
Total Points per recipe: 16

Chinese Pork and Noodle Stir-Fry

Serves 4

Preparation and cooking time:
22 minutes
Calories per serving: 300

Freezing: not recommended

This very easy stir-fry takes little more than twenty minutes to make.

120 g (4 oz) Chinese egg noodles
1/2 pork or chicken stock cube, dissolved in 150 ml (1/4 pint) hot water
1 tablespoon teriyaki marinade or soy sauce
1 teaspoon grated fresh root ginger
1 tablespoon cornflour
4 teaspoons sesame or vegetable oil
360 g (12 oz) lean leg or shoulder of pork, cut in strips
1 bunch of spring onions, sliced
90 g (3 oz) fine green beans, sliced
2 celery sticks, sliced finely
1 red pepper, de-seeded and sliced finely
1 carrot, sliced thinly
salt and freshly ground black pepper

1. Soak the egg noodles in boiling, lightly salted water for about 6 minutes, according to the packet instructions.
2. Meanwhile, mix together the stock, teriyaki marinade or soy sauce, ginger and cornflour.
3. Heat the oil in a wok or large frying-pan and add the pork. Cook over a high heat, stirring constantly, for 4–5 minutes.
4. Add all the vegetables and continue to stir-fry for a further 4–5 minutes. Stir in the stock mixture and cook for about 2 minutes, until thickened. Season to taste with salt and pepper.
5. Drain the noodles and add them to the stir-fry, tossing gently to incorporate. Spoon the stir-fry mixture on to four warm plates and serve immediately.

Cook's notes:
If you prefer, use 1/2 teaspoon of ground ginger instead of fresh. Use chicken instead of pork, for a change. This will change the Points per serving to 41/2 .

Points per serving: 5
Total Points per recipe: 20

v. tasty, but a bit dry. ? more tomatoes + some stock.

Pasta with Smoked Ham and Tomato Sauce

Serves 4

Preparation and cooking time:
22 minutes
Calories per serving: 305

Freezing: not recommended

The sauce for this dish can be made while the pasta cooks to give you a finished result in under 30 minutes!

240 g (8 oz) pasta shapes
2 teaspoons polyunsaturated margarine
1 bunch of spring onions, chopped finely
1 garlic clove, crushed
360 g (12 oz) tomatoes, skinned and chopped
120 g (4 oz) cooked smoked ham, chopped
120 g (4 oz) low-fat natural fromage frais
1 tablespoon chopped fresh oregano or basil or 1 teaspoon dried
1 tablespoon cornflour
4 teaspoons finely grated parmesan cheese
salt and freshly ground black pepper

1. Cook the pasta in plenty of lightly salted, boiling water until just cooked, about 8 minutes. It should retain a little 'bite'.
2. Meanwhile, melt the margarine in a saucepan and sauté the spring onions and garlic for about 3 minutes, until softened but not browned. Add the tomatoes and cook for 10 minutes over a low heat. Add the ham and cook for 2 minutes more. Remove from the heat.
3. Stir in the fromage frais and oregano or basil. Blend the cornflour with a little cold water and add to the saucepan. Return to the heat and cook gently, stirring constantly, until thickened and smooth. Season to taste.
4. Drain the pasta and add to the sauce, stirring to coat. Divide between four warmed plates and serve at once, topped with a teaspoon of parmesan cheese per portion.

Points per serving: 5
Total Points per recipe: 20

Garlic and Bacon Bubble and Squeak

Serves 4

Preparation and cooking time:
25 minutes
Calories per serving: 255

Freezing: recommended

Crisp bacon bits and garlic give a favourite leftover dish some extra flavour.

120 g (4 oz) lean back bacon
480 g (1 lb) cooked mashed potato
180 g (6 oz) lightly cooked cabbage, chopped
1 tablespoon chopped fresh parsley or chives
2 tablespoons skimmed milk
1 egg, beaten
2 tablespoons plain flour
2 tablespoons olive or vegetable oil
2 garlic cloves, crushed
salt and freshly ground black pepper

1. Grill the bacon rashers, turning once, until the fat stops dripping. Drain on kitchen paper and chop them finely.
2. Mix together the mashed potato, cabbage and bacon. Add the parsley or chives and season with salt and plenty of pepper. Mix in the milk and beaten egg to bind the mixture. Form into eight flat cakes. Sprinkle the flour on to a plate and dip in the cakes to coat them lightly.
3. Heat the oil in a large frying-pan and sauté the garlic for about a minute. Put the cakes into the pan and cook gently for about 5 minutes on each side, until thoroughly heated and golden brown.
4. Serve two cakes per person, sprinkled with a little extra black pepper.

Points per serving: 7
Total Points per recipe: 28

Pork Fillet with Roasted Autumn Fruits

Serves 4

Preparation and cooking time:
35 minutes
Calories per serving: 225

Freezing: not recommended

Lean pork fillet or 'tenderloin' tastes perfect when roasted with apples and pears.

30 g (1 oz) plain flour
1 teaspoon sage and apple seasoning or dried mixed herbs
480 g (1 lb) pork tenderloin
2 medium-size apples
2 medium-size pears
1 tablespoon lemon juice
salt and freshly ground black pepper

1. Preheat the oven to Gas Mark 6/200°C/400°F.
2. Sprinkle the flour, sage and apple seasoning or mixed herbs, salt and pepper on to a plate. Mix well.
3. Rinse the pork fillet, but do not pat it dry. Slice it thickly and then coat the pieces in the seasoned flour. Arrange them on a rack positioned over a roasting tin.
4. Quarter and core the apples and pears, without peeling them. Sprinkle them with lemon juice and place them next to the pork. Roast for 30–35 minutes, until the pork is cooked and the fruit is tender.

Points per serving: 6
Total Points per recipe: 24

Gammon and Vegetable Bean Pot

Serves 4

Preparation and cooking time:
40 minutes
Calories per serving: 340

Freezing: recommended

Try this delicious recipe, made with gammon, fresh vegetables and canned beans.

2 teaspoons olive or vegetable oil
1 garlic clove, crushed
1 large onion, chopped
2 celery sticks, sliced
1 turnip, chopped
2 carrots, sliced
420 g (14 oz) canned chopped tomatoes
450 g (15 oz) canned mixed beans in spicy sauce
360 g (12 oz) lean gammon, cubed
2 teaspoons paprika
1/2 ham or vegetable stock cube, dissolved in 150 ml (1/4 pint) boiling water
1 tablespoon chopped fresh parsley
2 tablespoons cornflour, blended with a little water
salt and freshly ground black pepper

1. Heat the oil in a flameproof casserole or large saucepan and sauté the garlic and onion for 2 minutes. Add the celery, turnip and carrots and cook, stirring, for 2–3 more minutes.
2. Add the tomatoes, mixed beans, gammon and paprika, stirring well, and then add the stock and parsley. Bring to the boil, cover and leave to simmer for 20–25 minutes.
3. Stir in the blended cornflour and cook gently for a minute more. Season with salt and pepper and serve.

Points per serving: 5½
Total Points per recipe: 22

Vegetarian Dishes

These vegetable-based recipes are ideal if you are watching your weight, regardless of whether you are a committed vegetarian or not. Full of colour and interesting textures, vegetables form an invaluable part of a healthy, balanced diet, providing important vitamins, minerals and fibre. They are low in fat too, which means that you can eat lots of them! So enjoy the variety these recipes offer: not only do they taste good, they are economical, too!

Vegetable Kebabs with Chick-pea Dip

Serves 4

Preparation and cooking time:
20 minutes
Calories per serving: 175

Freezing: not recommended

Grill or barbecue these tasty vegetable kebabs and then serve with a delicious puréed chick-pea dip.

240 g (8 oz) small new
    potatoes, cooked
1 red pepper, de-seeded and cut
    in squares
1 yellow pepper, de-seeded and
    cut in squares
120 g (4 oz) closed-cup
    mushrooms
2 courgettes, sliced thickly
1 medium-size aubergine,
    cubed
For the baste:
1 tablespoon lemon juice
1 tablespoon tomato purée
1 teaspoon ground coriander or
    mild curry powder
2 tablespoons low-fat natural
    yogurt
salt and freshly ground black
    pepper
For the chick-pea dip:
450 g (15 oz) canned chick-
    peas, rinsed and drained
4 spring onions, chopped
    roughly
2 tablespoons lemon juice
2 tablespoons low-fat natural
    yogurt
2 garlic cloves, crushed
1 tablespoon chopped fresh
    parsley
salt and freshly ground black
    pepper

1. Preheat the grill or barbecue. Thread all the vegetables on to skewers, alternating the different kinds.
2. Mix all the ingredients for the baste together and brush the baste over the kebabs. Grill or barbecue the kebabs for 5–8 minutes, turning and basting them from time to time.
3. Meanwhile, put all the ingredients for the chick–pea dip into a liquidiser or food processor. Blend for 15–20 seconds, until smooth. Serve with the vegetable kebabs.

Points per serving: 2
Total Points per recipe: 8

Speedy Vegetable Stir-Fry

Serves 4

Preparation and cooking time:
20 minutes
Calories per serving: 125

Freezing: not recommended

Canned Chinese-style
vegetables are used to make
this quick, convenient
stir-fry.

300 g (10 oz) smoked or firm
tofu, cubed
2 tablespoons light soy sauce
1 tablespoon sesame or
vegetable oil
1 large garlic clove, crushed
1 bunch of spring onions,
sliced finely
1 red pepper, de-seeded and
sliced finely
120 g (4 oz) broccoli, broken in
small florets
120 g (4 oz) Chinese leaves or
cabbage, shredded
360 g (12 oz) canned bamboo
shoots, drained
420 g (14 oz) canned bean
sprouts, drained
120 g (4 oz) oyster or button
mushrooms, sliced
1 teaspoon grated fresh root
ginger
1 teaspoon Chinese five-spice
powder
salt and freshly ground black
pepper

1. Put the tofu cubes in a bowl and add the soy sauce. Stir well
and set aside.
2. Heat the oil in a wok or large frying-pan. Add the garlic and
spring onions and stir-fry for a few seconds. Add the pepper and
broccoli and stir-fry for 3–4 minutes.
3. Add the Chinese leaves or cabbage, bamboo shoots, bean
sprouts, mushrooms, ginger and five-spice powder and stir-fry
for 2 more minutes. Add the tofu mixture and stir-fry for about
2 minutes, until heated through. Season with salt and pepper
and serve immediately.

Points per serving: 1½
Total Points per recipe: 6

Fresh Vegetable Platter, with Cheddar and Spring Onion Sauce

Serves 4

Preparation and cooking time:
20 minutes
Calories per serving: 130

Freezing: not recommended

V if using vegetarian cheese

A healthy plateful of lightly
cooked fresh vegetables tastes
even better with this tasty
savoury sauce.

240 g (8 oz) new carrots, sliced
120 g (4 oz) cauliflower, broken
in florets
120 g (4 oz) broccoli, broken in
florets
120 g (4 oz) dwarf green beans
180 g (6 oz) baby corn
2 courgettes, sliced
For the sauce:
2 tablespoons polyunsaturated
margarine
6 spring onions, chopped finely
2 tablespoons plain flour
300 ml (½ pint) skimmed milk
120 g (4 oz) mature reduced-fat
Cheddar cheese, grated
salt and freshly ground black
pepper

1. Place all the vegetables, except the courgettes, in a steamer
positioned over a pan of steadily boiling water and steam for
10 minutes. Add the courgettes. Steam for about 5 more minutes,
until the vegetables are cooked yet still crunchy. Alternatively,
cook the vegetables in a little boiling water, until tender.
2. Melt the margarine in a saucepan and add the spring onions.
Sauté for 5 minutes, to soften them. Stir in the flour and cook
gently over a low heat for a minute. Remove from the heat.
Gradually add the milk, return to the heat and bring to the boil,
stirring constantly, until thickened and smooth.
3. Add the cheese to the sauce and stir over a low heat until
melted. Season to taste with salt and pepper.
4. Divide the vegetables between four warm plates. Pour an equal
amount of sauce over each portion and serve at once.

Points per serving: 5½
Total Points per recipe: 22

Grilled Peppers with Melting Goat's Cheese

Serves 4

Preparation and cooking time: 20 minutes
Calories per serving: 200

Freezing: not recommended

 if using vegetarian cheese

Grilled peppers have become very popular and they taste even more delicious with a filling of soft goat's cheese.

2 large yellow peppers, halved and de-seeded
2 large red peppers, halved and de-seeded
2 large orange or green peppers, halved and de-seeded
180 g (6 oz) French goat's cheese, such as *chèvre blanc*
2 tablespoons olive oil
2 tablespoons lemon juice
salt and freshly ground black pepper

1. Preheat the grill to hot. Put the peppers, skin-side up, on a baking sheet. Grill for about 8 minutes, until just beginning to char. Turn them over.
2. Cut the cheese into 12 slices and place one piece in each pepper half. Grill for a further 2–3 minutes, until the cheese just begins to melt.
3. Meanwhile, mix together the olive oil and lemon juice. Season with salt and pepper and drizzle a teaspoon over each pepper half. Serve at once.

Points per serving: 5
Total Points per recipe: 20

Vegetable and Spicy-Bean Supper

Serves 4

Preparation and cooking time: 25 minutes
Calories per serving: 195

Freezing: not recommended

Feel free to substitute your favourite vegetables in this easy supper.

1 tablespoon olive or vegetable oil
1 onion, chopped
1 garlic clove, crushed
1 yellow or red pepper, de-seeded and chopped
2 courgettes, sliced
4 tomatoes, chopped
120 g (4 oz) mangetout or sugar-snap peas
1 teaspoon ground coriander
1 vegetable stock cube, dissolved in 60 ml (2 fl oz) boiling water
450 g (15 oz) canned mixed beans in spicy pepper sauce
120 g (4 oz) button mushrooms
120 g (4 oz) fresh spinach
6–8 basil leaves, torn in shreds
salt and freshly ground black pepper

1. Heat the oil in a wok or large frying-pan and sauté the onion until softened, about 3 minutes. Add the garlic, pepper and courgettes and cook, stirring, for 3–4 more minutes.
2. Add the tomatoes, mangetout or sugar-snap peas, coriander, vegetable stock and mixed beans. Heat, stirring occasionally, for about 5 minutes. Add the mushrooms and spinach and cook for 2–3 minutes more, until the spinach has wilted.
3. Season with salt and pepper, stir in the basil and serve at once.

Cook's note:
If you can't find mixed beans in spicy pepper sauce, use canned mixed pulses, spiced up with a shake or two of Tabasco sauce.

Points per serving: 2½
Total Points per recipe: 10

Spanish Omelette Wedges

Serves 4

Preparation and cooking time:
35 minutes
Calories per serving: 205

Freezing: not recommended

V if using vegetarian cheese

Slices of Spanish omelette
or *tortilla* taste delicious eaten
warm, served with a fresh
mixed salad. This is perfect
for a light lunch or evening
meal.

1 tablespoon olive oil
1 large onion, chopped
1 garlic clove, crushed
360 g (12 oz) cooked potatoes,
  cubed
1 tablespoon chopped fresh
  parsley
2 eggs
2 tablespoons skimmed milk
60 g (2 oz) mature Cheddar
  cheese, grated
salt and freshly ground black
  pepper

1. Heat the oil in a medium-sized, heavy-based frying-pan. Add
the onion and garlic and sauté them gently for about 5 minutes.
2. Add the potatoes and continue to cook, stirring occasionally, for
4–5 minutes. Season well with salt and pepper. Stir in the parsley.
Continue to cook gently, without stirring, for about 3 minutes,
until the potatoes begin to brown and set on the base.
3. Preheat the grill.
4. Beat the eggs and milk together and add to the frying-pan,
loosening the potatoes slightly to allow the egg mixture through.
Sprinkle the cheese over the surface and cook gently until set
(about 3 minutes). Transfer to the grill to brown the surface.
Leave the omelette to cool in the pan for about 5 minutes.
5. Cut the omelette into quarters and serve warm.

Points per serving: 4
Total Points per recipe: 16

Parmesan and Mushroom Risotto

Serves 4

Preparation and cooking time:
40 minutes
Calories per serving: 295

Freezing: not recommended

V if using vegetarian
parmesan

Quick, easy and very tasty,
this recipe is ideal for lunch
or as a supper dish.

1 tablespoon olive oil
180 g (6 oz) risotto or
  long-grain rice
1 large onion, chopped
1 garlic clove, crushed
2 celery sticks, sliced
1 red or yellow pepper,
  de-seeded and chopped
30 g (1 oz) sun-dried tomatoes,
  sliced
240 g (8 oz) mushrooms, sliced
2 vegetable stock cubes,
  dissolved in 900 ml (1½
  pints) boiling water
1 tablespoon chopped fresh
  herbs, e.g. basil, oregano,
  marjoram, chives or parsley
60 g (2 oz) finely grated
  parmesan cheese
salt and freshly ground black
  pepper

1. Heat the oil in a large frying-pan or wok. Add the rice and sauté,
without browning, for about 5 minutes. Add the onion, garlic, celery,
pepper, tomatoes and mushrooms. Cook, stirring, for 5 more minutes.
2. Pour the hot stock into the pan and bring to the boil. Reduce the
heat and simmer gently, stirring occasionally, for about 20 minutes,
until the rice is tender and the stock has been absorbed. Add a little
extra water if the rice is not fully cooked before the liquid has been
absorbed.
3. Add the herbs and half the parmesan cheese to the risotto and
then season with salt and pepper. Serve at once, sprinkled with the
remaining cheese.

Cook's notes:
Risotto or arborio rice is the best for this recipe; it turns deliciously
creamy as it cooks and absorbs the stock. Choose sun-dried
tomatoes in a packet, rather than those bottled in olive oil.
Alternatively, use 2 chopped fresh tomatoes. For a special occasion,
try using a selection of unusual mushrooms.

Points per serving: 5
Total Points per recipe: 20

Celery and Tomato Crumble

Serves 4

Preparation and cooking time:
45 minutes
Calories per serving: 415

Freezing: recommended

 if using vegetarian cheese

Celery, onion, carrot and
tomatoes are topped with
a delicious cheese and oat
crumble in this tasty
vegetarian dish. Serve with
a crisp green salad.

1 tablespoon vegetable oil
1 onion, sliced thinly
6 celery sticks, sliced thinly
420 g (14 oz) canned chopped
   tomatoes with herbs
1 carrot, chopped finely
450 g (15 oz) canned mixed
   beans in mild chilli sauce
1 vegetable stock cube,
   dissolved in 150 ml (1/4 pint)
   boiling water
1 tablespoon tomato purée
1/2 teaspoon cumin seeds
   (optional)
2 tablespoons cornflour,
   blended with a little cold
   water
For the topping:
60 g (2 oz) plain flour
60 g (2 oz) rolled oats
2 tablespoons polyunsaturated
   margarine
60 g (2 oz) mature Cheddar
   cheese, grated
salt and freshly ground black
   pepper

1. Preheat the oven to Gas Mark 6/200°C/400°F.
2. Heat the vegetable oil in a saucepan and sauté the onion and celery until softened. Add the tomatoes, carrot, mixed beans, stock, tomato purée and cumin seeds (if using). Bring to the boil and reduce the heat. Simmer, uncovered, for 5 minutes.
3. Meanwhile, to make the topping, put the flour and rolled oats into a mixing bowl and add a pinch of salt. Rub in the margarine until the mixture resembles fine breadcrumbs; then stir in the grated cheese.
4. Stir the blended cornflour into the tomato mixture and heat, stirring, until the sauce thickens. Cook gently for a minute and then season to taste with salt and pepper. Transfer to a large ovenproof dish. Sprinkle the crumble mixture evenly over the top. Bake for 20 minutes, until golden brown. Serve at once.

Cook's note:
If you can't find mixed beans in a mild chilli sauce, try using a can of mixed pulses and add 1/2 teaspoon of chilli powder and an extra tablespoon of tomato purée to the recipe.

Points per serving: 7 1/2
Total Points per recipe: 30

Vegetable and Bean Tortillas

Serves 4

Preparation and cooking time:
45 minutes
Calories per serving: 375

Freezing: not recommended

Ⓥ if using vegetarian cheese

Buy Mexican-style soft
tortillas from the supermarket
or the delicatessen. They taste
superb in this excellent
vegetarian recipe.

4 teaspoons vegetable oil
1 onion, chopped
1–2 garlic cloves, crushed
1 red pepper, de-seeded and
  chopped
1 small aubergine, chopped
120 g (4 oz) mushrooms, sliced
180 g (6 oz) canned chick-peas
  or red kidney beans, rinsed
  and drained
1 teaspoon chilli powder
1 tablespoon chopped fresh
  coriander
4 × 15 cm (6–inch) soft tortillas
120 g (4 oz) Cheddar cheese,
  grated
salt and freshly ground black
  pepper
fresh coriander sprigs, to
  garnish

1. Preheat the oven to Gas Mark 4/180°C/350°F.
2. Heat the oil in a large frying-pan and sauté the onion and garlic,
until softened. Add the pepper, aubergine, mushrooms, chick-peas
or red kidney beans and chilli powder. Cook for about 5 minutes
more. Add the coriander to the frying-pan and mix well. Season
with salt and pepper.
3. Lay the tortillas on a work surface and divide the filling equally
between them. Roll up and place in a baking dish. Scatter the
grated cheese on top and bake in the oven for 20–25 minutes.
4. Serve the tortillas garnished with sprigs of fresh coriander.

Cook's note:
Instead of chick-peas or kidney beans, use 180 g (6 oz) of canned or
frozen sweetcorn instead. Points per serving will be 6½.

Points per serving: 7
Total Points per recipe: 28

Vegetable and Macaroni Cheese Bake

Serves 4

Preparation and cooking time:
45 minutes
Calories per serving: 325

Freezing: recommended

Ⓥ if using vegetarian cheese

Create this delicious midweek meal with macaroni and
fresh vegetables and a light
cheese sauce.

180 g (6 oz) macaroni
90 g (3 oz) green beans, sliced *onion*
1 courgette, sliced
1 small red or yellow pepper,
  de-seeded and sliced
120 g (4 oz) cauliflower or
  broccoli, broken in small
  florets
450 ml (¾ pint) skimmed milk
3 tablespoons cornflour
90 g (3 oz) mature Cheddar
  cheese
salt and freshly ground black
  pepper

1. Preheat the oven to Gas Mark 5/190°C/375°F.
2. Cook the macaroni in plenty of boiling, lightly salted water for
about 10 minutes, until just tender. Meanwhile, cook the vegetables
in a small amount of boiling, lightly salted water for 3–4 minutes;
drain well.
3. While the macaroni and vegetables are cooking, put the milk
and cornflour in a saucepan and stir until blended. Heat, stirring
constantly with a small wire whisk or wooden spoon, until thickened
and smooth. Remove from the heat and add most of the cheese,
stirring until it melts. Season with salt and pepper.
4. Drain the macaroni and add the cheese sauce, stirring well. Add
the vegetables and stir well again. Transfer to a shallow ovenproof
baking dish and sprinkle with the reserved cheese. Bake for
15–20 minutes, until the cheese melts and turns golden brown.

Points per serving: 5
Total Points per recipe: 20

Grease oblong serving dish well. (handwritten)

Cheese and Tomato Bake

Serves 4

Preparation and cooking time:
45 minutes
Calories per serving: 335

Freezing: not recommended

V if using vegetarian cheese
and free-range eggs

The perfect answer for an
economical midweek meal,
this dish can be assembled in
moments with the help of
your food processor or
blender. Serve with salad or
vegetables, but remember that
a dressing adds extra Points!

4 teaspoons polyunsaturated
    margarine
180 g (6 oz) white bread, torn
    in pieces
1 small onion, chopped finely
120 g (4 oz) mature Cheddar
    cheese, grated
2 eggs
450 ml (³/4 pint) skimmed milk
2 tomatoes, sliced
salt and freshly ground black
    pepper

1. Preheat the oven to Gas Mark 5/190°C/375°F. Grease a 1.2-litre
(2-pint) baking dish with ¹/2 teaspoon of the margarine.
2. Put the bread in a blender or food processor. Process to make fine
breadcrumbs and then tip into the baking dish.
3. Heat the remaining margarine in a small saucepan and sauté the
onion, until softened. Mix with the breadcrumbs in the baking dish
and add half the cheese.
4. Blend or beat together the eggs and milk and season with salt
and pepper. Pour over the breadcrumb mixture.
5. Arrange the sliced tomatoes over the top of the breadcrumb
mixture and sprinkle with the reserved cheese. Bake for
35 minutes, until risen and golden brown.

Points per serving: 6¹/2
Total Points per recipe: 26

Needs vegetables too — not enough (handwritten)

Stuffed Baked Marrow

Serves 4

Preparation and cooking time:
45 minutes
Calories per serving: 195

Freezing: not recommended

V if using vegetarian cheese

A tasty mixture of creamy
risotto rice, celery and
mushrooms – flavoured with
peppery fresh basil and topped
with cheese – fills hollowed-
out marrow slices. Serve with
salad and count the extra
Points if you use a dressing.

1 medium-size marrow,
    sliced thickly
2 teaspoons olive oil
4 spring onions, sliced finely
1 celery stick, chopped finely
2 tomatoes, chopped
120 g (4 oz) button
    mushrooms, sliced
180 g (6 oz) cooked risotto rice
1 tablespoon chopped fresh
    basil or 1 teaspoon dried
120 g (4 oz) mature reduced-fat
    Cheddar cheese, grated
salt and freshly ground black
    pepper

1. Preheat the oven to Gas Mark 4/180°C/350°F.
2. Using a dessertspoon, scoop out the seeds and pulp from
the marrow. Arrange the slices in an ovenproof baking dish.
3. Heat the olive oil in a small frying-pan and gently sauté
the spring onions, celery, tomatoes and mushrooms for about
3–4 minutes, until softened.
4. In a mixing bowl, combine the rice and cooked vegetables.
Season with salt, pepper and basil. Pile this mixture into the
scooped-out marrow. Sprinkle the cheese evenly over the surface.
5. Bake for 20–25 minutes, until the cheese is golden brown and
bubbling.

Cook's note:
If you can't buy marrow, pack the rice mixture into scooped-out
courgettes or aubergines.

Points per serving: 3¹/2
Total Points per recipe: 14

Desserts

Just because you are watching your weight, it doesn't mean that you have to miss out on dessert. Quite the contrary! Besides satisfying your sweet tooth, these delicious recipes are the perfect way to finish off a meal, being low in fat and considerate of Calories. In fact, most of them are extremely nutritious and healthy, providing important vitamins and minerals that help to make up a sensible, balanced diet. So why not try some of these ingenious ideas to round off your meals in the most delightful way?

Strawberries with Dark Chocolate Sauce

Serves 4

Preparation and cooking time:
10 minutes
Calories per serving: 140

Freezing: not recommended

Strawberries taste very indulgent when dipped into this wonderful hot chocolate sauce: simple, yet scrumptious!

480 g (1 lb) fresh strawberries
For the chocolate sauce:
2 teaspoons cocoa powder
2 teaspoons cornflour
150 ml (¼ pint) skimmed milk
60 g (2 oz) dark chocolate,
    broken in pieces
1 tablespoon golden syrup

1. Place all the ingredients for the chocolate sauce into a small saucepan. Heat gently, stirring constantly with a small whisk, until the sauce is thickened and smooth.
2. Divide the strawberries between four serving dishes and then pour the chocolate sauce into four small pots to serve with them.

Cook's note:
There's no need to hull the strawberries: the stalks make useful 'handles' for dipping the fruit into the hot sauce!

Points per serving: 3½
Total Points per recipe: 14

Raspberry Meringue Puddings

Serves 4

Preparation and cooking time:
15 minutes
Calories per serving: 120

Freezing: not recommended

 if using free-range eggs

Fresh or frozen raspberries can be used in this easy dessert.

4 small slices of Calorie-reduced bread
480 g (1 lb) raspberries, defrosted if frozen
finely grated zest and juice of 1 medium-size orange
4 teaspoons powdered artificial sweetener
2 egg whites
2 tablespoons caster sugar

1. Preheat the oven to Gas Mark 4/180°C/350°F.
2. Cut four circles from the sliced bread and fit them into the bases of four individual heatproof dishes. Divide the raspberries between the dishes. Mix the orange zest and juice with the powdered sweetener and sprinkle over the desserts.
3. Whisk the egg whites in a grease-free bowl, using a scrupulously clean whisk or electric beaters, until soft peaks form. Add the sugar and whisk again until stiff and glossy.
4. Pile an equal amount of meringue on top of the raspberries. Bake in the oven for 5–6 minutes, or until the meringue is golden brown and crisp.

Points per serving: 2
Total Points per recipe: 8

Canteloupe Melon with Ginger and Honey Yogurt

Serves 4

Preparation and cooking time:
15 minutes
Calories per serving: 115

Freezing: not recommended

Try natural yogurt with a little grated fresh root ginger and a spoonful of honey: it tastes marvellous with melon.

1 large cantaloupe or charentais melon
2 teaspoons finely grated fresh root ginger
300 ml (½ pint) low-fat natural yogurt
8 teaspoons clear honey
fresh mint sprigs, to decorate

1. Cut the melon into four equal pieces. Peel and slice the flesh and arrange the slices on four serving plates.
2. Mix the ginger into the yogurt, with half the honey, and spoon over the melon. Drizzle a teaspoon of honey over each portion and decorate with mint leaves.

Cook's note:
Try a combination of 360 g (12 oz) fresh strawberries and a small melon, for a delicious change.

Points per serving: 2½
Total Points per recipe: 10

Grilled Fresh Pineapple with Nutmeg and Cinnamon Topping

Serves 4

Preparation and cooking time:
15 minutes
Calories per serving: 160

Freezing: not recommended

Grill some juicy slices of fresh pineapple and then serve them with some spiced-up fromage frais for an easy, delicious dessert!

1 medium-size fresh pineapple
8 teaspoons demerara sugar
240 g (8 oz) low-fat natural fromage frais
$^1/_2$ teaspoon finely grated nutmeg
$^1/_2$ teaspoon ground cinnamon powdered artificial sweetener, to taste

1. Preheat the grill to hot. Prepare the pineapple by cutting off the spiky top and then peeling it with a sharp knife. Cut the flesh into eight slices.
2. Place the pineapple slices on the grill pan and sprinkle a teaspoon of sugar on each slice. Grill on one side only, until golden and bubbling.
3. Meanwhile, mix together the fromage frais, nutmeg and cinnamon. Add a little sweetener, according to taste.
4. Serve two slices of pineapple per person, accompanied by the flavoured fromage frais.

Cook's note:
Use 1 teaspoon of finely grated fresh ginger or $^1/_2$ teaspoon of ground ginger in place of nutmeg, if preferred.

Points per serving: 3
Total Points per recipe: 12

Summer Berry Brûlée

Serves 4

Preparation and cooking time:
15 minutes
Calories per serving: 150

Freezing: not recommended

 **if using vegetarian cheese**

Fresh berries taste marvellous in this deliciously simple summer dessert; in winter just use frozen berries!

480 g (1 lb) mixed soft fruit, e.g. strawberries, raspberries, blackberries, tayberries, etc.
2 tablespoons water
powdered artificial sweetener, to taste
240 g (8 oz) low-fat soft cheese
1 teaspoon lemon juice
4 tablespoons low-fat natural yogurt
$^1/_2$ teaspoon vanilla essence
8 teaspoons demerara sugar

1. Slice the strawberries, if large, and mix with all the remaining fruit. Heat very gently with the water in a saucepan, until the juices just begin to run, about 2 minutes. Add sweetener to taste and then spoon into four individual heatproof dishes. Cool and chill thoroughly.
2. Beat the soft cheese until creamy and then add the lemon juice, yogurt and vanilla essence. Spoon over the fruit, levelling the surface to cover completely. Chill.
3. Preheat the grill. Sprinkle 2 teaspoons of sugar evenly over the surface of each dessert. Place under the grill for about 2 minutes, until bubbling and golden brown, taking care not to let them burn. Leave to cool for a few minutes, and then serve, or chill for serving later.

Points per serving: 3
Total Points per recipe: 12

Pink Grapefruit and Honeydew Salad

Serves 4

Preparation and cooking time:
15 minutes
Calories per serving: 75

Freezing: not recommended

**Refreshing pink grapefruit
tastes fantastic with
honeydew melon in a light,
minted honey syrup.**

1 lemon
90 ml (3 fl oz) water
2 tablespoons clear honey
fresh mint sprigs
1/2 medium-size honeydew
   melon, or any other melon,
   except watermelon
2 medium-size pink grapefruit,
   segmented

1. Thinly pare the rind from the lemon, using a potato peeler, and put it into a small saucepan, with the water and honey. Add a tablespoon of lemon juice. Heat and simmer gently for 5 minutes. Remove from the heat, add a few sprigs of mint and allow to cool.
2. Scoop the flesh from the honeydew melon, using a melon baller, or cut it into chunks.
3. Strain the cooled syrup into a serving dish, discarding the lemon rind and mint sprigs. Add the grapefruit and melon, stirring gently to mix. Chill until ready to serve, decorated with more sprigs of fresh mint.

Points per serving: 1 1/2
Total Points per recipe: 6

Quick Citrus Trifles

Serves 4

Preparation and chilling time:
20 minutes
Calories per serving: 235

Freezing: not recommended

**Ten minutes to make and ten
minutes to chill is all you
need for these speedy citrus
desserts.**

1 lemon
2 × 125 g pots very-low-fat
   orange or mandarin yogurt
240 g (8 oz) ricotta or low-fat
   soft cheese
2 medium-size oranges
2 meringue nests
4 sponge fingers
powdered artificial sweetener,
   to taste

1. Cut the lemon in half. Cut one half into thin slices and reserve for decoration.
2. Mix the yogurt and ricotta or low-fat soft cheese together, until blended. Grate the rind from the oranges and the remaining lemon half and stir into the mixture.
3. Remove all the peel and membrane from the oranges using a sharp, serrated knife and then segment the fruit. Chop the flesh roughly and add to the yogurt mixture. Squeeze the juice from the lemon half and stir into the yogurt mixture.
4. Roughly crumble the meringue nests and sponge fingers into the mixture and stir well. Add a little powdered sweetener, if required. Divide between four serving glasses and chill for at least 10 minutes before serving. Decorate with the reserved lemon slices.

Points per serving: 5 1/2
Total Points per recipe: 22

Drop Scones with Ice Cream and Butterscotch Sauce

Serves 4

Preparation and cooking time:
20 minutes
Calories per serving: 255

Freezing: not recommended

V if using free-range eggs

These small pancakes taste superb with a dollop of low-fat ice cream and a trickle of hot butterscotch sauce.

120 g (4 oz) vanilla fat-reduced
    ice cream, to serve
For the batter:
120 g (4 oz) plain flour
¹/₂ teaspoon baking powder
a pinch of salt
1 egg, beaten
210 ml (7 fl oz) skimmed milk
low-fat cooking spray
For the sauce:
1 tablespoon polyunsaturated
    margarine
2 tablespoons golden syrup
2 tablespoons caster sugar
1 teaspoon lemon juice

1. Put the flour, baking powder, salt, egg and milk into a large bowl and whisk together until smooth.
2. Heat a heavy-based frying-pan and spray once with the cooking spray. Add tablespoons of batter to the pan to make drop scones. Cook gently, turning them over as bubbles begin to appear on the surface. Cook the other side for about 1 minute more. Transfer to sheets of kitchen paper as they cook and then keep them, covered, in a warm place.
3. To make the sauce, gently heat the margarine, syrup, sugar and lemon juice together until dissolved, stirring constantly. Do not allow the mixture to boil. Serve the drop scones with the hot sauce and ice cream.

Points per serving: 4
Total Points per recipe: 16

Autumn Blackberry Chill

Serves 4

Preparation and chilling time:
30 minutes
Calories per serving: 165

Freezing: not recommended

 if using vegetarian cheese

Fromage frais and fruit yogurt transform blackberries and toasted porridge oats into a real treat!

60 g (2 oz) porridge oats
360 g (12 oz) fresh or frozen
  blackberries, defrosted
120 g (4 oz) very-low-fat
  natural fromage frais
120 g (4 oz) low-fat soft cheese
125 g very-low-fat blackberry
  yogurt
½ teaspoon vanilla essence
  powdered artificial sweetener
  fresh mint leaves, to decorate
  (optional)

1. Dry-fry the porridge oats in a heavy-based frying-pan stirring and tossing occasionally to toast lightly. Allow to cool.
2. Reserve a few blackberries for decoration. Spoon half the remaining blackberries into four serving glasses. Beat the fromage frais and low-fat soft cheese together and then mix in the yogurt and vanilla essence. Fold in the toasted oats and blackberries, and add a little powdered sweetener, according to taste.
3. Spoon the mixture into the glasses and then chill the desserts for at least 20 minutes, or until ready to serve. Decorate with the reserved blackberries and mint leaves (if using).

Cook's notes:
Use raspberries or strawberries instead of blackberries, choosing the appropriately flavoured yogurt to match. If you like, use a total of 240 g (8 oz) of fromage frais and omit the low-fat soft cheese. The Points per serving will be the same.

Points per serving: 3
Total Points per recipe: 12

Choca Pots

Serves 4

Preparation time: 35 minutes
Calories per serving: 175

Freezing: not recommended

 if using free-range eggs

A *little* self–indulgence will do you no harm at all, so try one of these smooth, creamy chocolate pots!

60 g (2 oz) plain chocolate,
  broken in pieces
2 teaspoons cocoa powder
1 tablespoon cornflour
8 tablespoons skimmed milk
1 tablespoon caster sugar
6 tablespoons whipping cream
2 egg whites

1. Put the chocolate in a small, heavy-based saucepan, with the cocoa powder, cornflour and 6 tablespoons of milk. Heat gently, stirring the mixture constantly, until thick, melted and smooth.
2. Pour the chocolate mixture into a bowl and stir in the sugar and remaining milk. Cool for about 10 minutes, stirring frequently to prevent a skin from forming.
3. Whip the cream in a chilled bowl until it holds its shape. Fold most of it through the chocolate mixture, reserving a little for decoration.
4. In a grease-free bowl, whisk the egg whites, using a scrupulously clean whisk or electric beaters, until stiff peaks form. Stir 2 tablespoons of the egg white into the chocolate mixture to 'slacken' it and then gently fold in the remainder. Divide between four small pots or serving glasses and then cover and chill for at least 20 minutes.
5. Top each dessert with a spoonful of the reserved cream, to decorate.

Points per serving: 5½
Total Points per recipe: 22

Light Lemony Pudding

Serves 4

Preparation and cooking time:
40 minutes
Calories per serving: 245

Freezing: not recommended

 if using free-range eggs

This lovely lemon pudding is the perfect recipe for using up some slightly stale bread – to great effect!

8 slices of low-calorie bread
45 g (1½ oz) caster sugar
450 ml (¾ pint) skimmed milk
2 eggs
1 teaspoon vanilla essence
2 lemons
1 tablespoon cornflour
120 ml (4 fl oz) orange juice
powdered artificial sweetener,
  to taste

1. Preheat the oven to Gas Mark 4/180°C/350°F.
2. Tear the slices of bread into small pieces and put them into four individual heatproof dishes.
3. Reserve a tablespoon of sugar. Beat together the milk, eggs, remaining sugar and vanilla essence. Finely grate the zest and squeeze the juice from 1 lemon. Add the zest to the milk mixture and pour an equal amount into each dish. Reserve the lemon juice.
4. Slice the remaining lemon very thinly and arrange two or three slices over each dessert. Sprinkle with the reserved sugar. Bake for about 25–30 minutes, until set.
5. To make the sauce, blend the cornflour with the reserved lemon juice and the orange juice in a small saucepan. Heat, stirring, until thickened and smooth. Remove from the heat and add sweetener to taste. Run a knife around the edge of each dish and turn out the puddings. Serve with the sauce.

Points per serving: 3½
Total Points per recipe: 14

Index